MAKING PEACE

A Catholic Guide to
Turning Conflict into Grace

A Catholic Guide to
Turning Conflict into Grace

ED GAFFNEY & TERRI SORTOR

TWENTY-THIRD PUBLICATIONS

185 WILLOW STREET • PO BOX 180 • MYSTIC, CT 06355
TEL: 1-800-321-0411 • FAX: 1-800-572-0788
E-MAIL: ttpubs@aol.com • www.twentythirdpublications.com

The poems in the sections "Prayer & Reflection" are original works by Ed Gaffney.

Scripture quotations are from the *New Revised Standard Version of the Bible*, © 1989, by the Division of Christian Education of the National Council of Churches of Christ in the U.S.A. Used by permission. All rights reserved.

Twenty-Third Publications
A Division of Bayard
185 Willow Street
P.O. Box 180
Mystic, CT 06355
(860) 536-2611 or (800) 321-0411
www.twentythirdpublications.com
ISBN:1-58595-374-1

Library of Congress Catalog Card Number: 2004098879
Printed in the U.S.A.

Acknowledgments

The writers wish to express their gratitude to:

Ken Sande and Peacemaker Ministries for their inspired work upon which this study guide is based, as well as for their generous support, their ecumenical sensitivity, and their comprehensive training in Christian conciliation.

The Catholic Diocese of Colorado Springs for its generosity in allowing us to pursue extensive instruction and training through Peacemaker Ministries.

Dave Edling of Peacemaker Ministries for his constant encouragement, prayers, practical advice, and insightful editing of this book—and especially for his patience during this process. Dave's life is a living witness to the principles of peacemaking.

Our spouses and families for their patient and prayerful support during the many hours of the preparation of this book.

References found in the text to "Sande" are to the third edition of *The Peacemaker* (Baker Books; www.bakerbooks.com).

More information about Peacemaker Ministries can be found at www.hispeace.org.

Contents

Blessed are the peacemakers,
all humble people everywhere
who strive to live peacefully,
even through the greatest difficulties,
challenges, and conflicts of life.

Introduction

Peace be with you. It is I, do not be afraid.

With these words, Jesus reassured his disciples as they were sitting in their small boat, being tossed about in a storm. With these same words he comforts us and communicates his mission on earth.

Our trip is storm-tossed, too, and the waves are highest when conflict rages in our lives. We feel threatened by the winds of discord and the whitecaps of rage. As strong emotions assail us, we feel cast adrift and abandoned to the elements of human emotion. We, too, look to Jesus to rescue us and reassure us, to strengthen us and guide us to the safe and distant shore.

We wonder, "Where can we find refuge?" and "What good is our faith in the midst of such fury?"

Making Peace: A Catholic Guide to Turning Conflict into Grace offers an answer to these questions. It explains a way to take our faith and use it to respond to the storms of conflict in our lives. Using a simple—but not easy—four-step process that begins in Chapter 4, this book connects our call to holiness to the opportunity to demonstrate our faith in action during stressful and challenging conflict situations.

There are five fundamental principles that form the foundation of this process:

1. *The centrality of Christ.* Unless we truly believe that through Jesus Christ we "live and move and have our being," we will never experience the peace with others that is beyond all understanding. We need to seek God's grace as well as his will for us in these conflict situations.

2. *The role of our faith.* We believe that conflict gives us a great opportunity to witness to our faith, to "put flesh" on the Word, and provide a counter-cultural response to difficult situations. Scripture says that others will know us by the love we demonstrate for one another. Responding to conflict in a way that is different than what the world would expect exemplifies our commitment to Christ.

3. *The sacramental life of the Church.* As Catholics, we celebrate the most important events of our lives through the sacraments of our Church. By receiving the sacraments often, we avail ourselves of the grace to meet all of life's challenges. This determination to take full advantage of our sacramental life enables us—even, we might say, emboldens us—to follow Christ more closely and imitate him in his dying and rising, in every area of our lives.

4. *The necessity of spiritual counsel.* Conflicts arise when our sinfulness influences our response to a situation. Instead, we need to guide each other through difficult times with the truths of our Catholic faith. This includes lovingly confronting one another in truth and discerning God's will for our lives.

5. *The comprehensiveness of our faith.* Rooted in Scripture and tradition, the depth of the Catholic faith is revealed in the holy Bible, the teachings of the magisterium throughout the centuries (found in resources such as the papal encyclicals and documents of the Vatican Councils), canon law, and the *Catechism of the Catholic Church.* Combined with the sacraments, we have a firm foundation for witnessing to God's love and truth in every situation of life—and especially during conflict.

While conflict is not something that people typically embrace, our hope is that you will have a different attitude toward it by the end of this book. By using the suggestions found here, and calling on the help of the Holy Spirit, we can turn potentially unpleasant experiences into occasions of grace.

How to Use This Book

Making Peace can be used in an adult study group, a religious education program, with parish staff, or by individuals. The material found here is valuable in dealing with conflicts that occur within Church structures and situations, but equally valuable for conflicts that arise in our lives outside the parish, whether in our family, work, or other relationships and activities.

This book will guide you through a sequential process in which each session builds on the last with the intention of forming hearts to respond to conflict in a faith-filled way. Each session contains a lesson, questions for reflection and/or discussion, a prayer, and a blank page for notes.

The questions for reflection and discussion are developed for readers to gain a deeper understanding of their own attitudes and responses as well as to help them understand and appreciate others in a deeper way. The prayer can be used for quiet reflection, or as an opening prayer or closing prayer with groups.

If you are using this book in a group setting, participants are encouraged to come to each class having read the session's lesson beforehand and prepared their responses to the questions for sharing. Reading the lesson aloud early in the session can help to focus the group and assist them in recalling the content to be considered. Pausing during the reading to allow discussion and questions is another effective strategy.

It's helpful to have on hand the two major resources used in this book: a Bible and the *Catechism of the Catholic Church*. When these are referenced, the resource could be consulted to provide further background and clarification.

We recommend that this book be read and studied before one is engaged in conflict. Scripture teaches us to "put on the armor of

Christ" at the beginning of each day, and not wait until we are under attack. As disciples of Christ, we believe that reconciling our conflicts and broken relationships with others is not optional. This calls for a conversion in our own hearts in order to successfully resolve these situations.

Finally, developing a commitment to prayer and reflection is the very best way to discover God's will and remain open to the work of the Holy Spirit in our hearts.

Prayer & Reflection

O God, who taught the hearts of the faithful by the light of the Holy Spirit, grant that, by the gift of the same Spirit, we may be truly wise, and ever rejoice in your consolation. We ask this through Christ our Lord. Amen.

1

Our Call to Holiness

It was a quiet, star-lit night, perfect for sitting on the porch swing and contemplating the complexities of life—and Fran's life was certainly complex. After twenty-five high stress years in banking, she welcomed what she thought would be a quiet and routine period of life. Yet it was anything but. Her daughter's unexpected accident had thrust Fran back into childrearing, with the daily care of her two energetic teenage grandchildren. "This is not exactly what I had in mind," she thought.

For anyone who has experienced such an abrupt turn, it's natural to raise some fundamental questions. And haven't all of us at one time or another asked the question: "God, what do you want of me?" To quote the most prolific of poets, author unknown, the shortest poem in the English language is

I?

or, for those who insist that poetry rhyme,

I,
Why?

These and other fundamental questions of existence may bewilder those who are not conscious of their faith journey, but as

Catholics, we should have a clearer sense of our purpose and direction. During a press conference after it was announced that Mother Teresa had won the Nobel Peace Prize, a cynical reporter asked her, "You have been called a 'living saint' and a 'holy woman.' What do you have to say about that?" Mother Teresa gazed steadily at the man and replied gently, "It is the same for you as it is for me; we are all called to holiness." The reporter did not ask any more questions.

Basic to our Catholic faith is our individual and communal call to holiness. This begins at the moment of baptism when we become members of the Church, which is holy in Christ. Understanding and deeply embracing this call is critical if we are taking God's will for us seriously.

As Catholics, we tend not to be intentional in our journey toward holiness. In fact, we probably spend more time planning what to wear or what to eat than we do in planning our growth toward holiness. This morning, for example, did you spend more time preparing your exterior (body) or your interior (spirit) for the day ahead?

As individuals, this call is dependent on a deeply personal relationship with Jesus Christ. As members of the human community, our communal call requires us to be concerned about the salvation of our brothers and sisters in Christ. We respond by striving to support, encourage, and challenge one another as we go along on our journey of faith.

We see this call to holiness articulated in Scripture, the Code of Canon Law, the documents of the Second Vatican Council, and the *Catechism of the Catholic Church* (CCC):

> Blessed be the God and Father of our Lord Jesus Christ, who has blessed us in Christ with every spiritual blessing in the heavenly places, just as he chose us in Christ before the foundation of the world to be holy and blameless before him in love. (Eph 1:3–4)

> All the Christian faithful must make an effort...to live a holy life....(Canon 210)

God has, however, willed to make everyone holy...to make them into a people who might acknowledge him and serve him in holiness. (*Lumen Gentium*, The People of God, 9)

All Christians in any state or walk of life are called to the perfection of charity. (CCC, 2013)

It is clear, just from these brief references, that God expects us to respond generously and deeply to this call. We must remember, though, that our journey of faith is not to be walked alone. God's plan intends a communal response as well; we are our "brother's keeper" (Gen 4:9).

Even by [our] secular activity [we] must aid one another to greater holiness of life, so that the world may be filled with the Spirit of Christ and may then more effectively attain its destiny in justice, in love, and in peace. (*Lumen Gentium*, 36)

If it is our destiny to grow in holiness and to bring about justice, love, and peace in our world, how do we equip ourselves for this journey? Certainly, taking time to pray and reflect on the Scriptures would begin to center our focus upon God and his will for us. But how do we put flesh on the Word in our day-to-day living? How do we ensure that we are formed by our Catholic faith and not by a secular society that is often at odds with our values and beliefs?

Some activities to consider may include:

- taking time to pray for the gifts of the Spirit (wisdom, understanding, knowledge, counsel, piety, fortitude, fear of the Lord) (CCC, 1831; cf. Is 11:1–2);
- embracing the cardinal virtues (prudence, justice, fortitude, temperance) (CCC, 1834–38);
- following the Ten Commandments;
- embodying the fruits of the Spirit (charity, joy, peace, patience, kindness, goodness, generosity, gentleness, faithfulness, modesty, self-control, chastity) (CCC, 1832; cf. Gal 5:22);

- living true Christian love: "Love is patient; love is kind; love is not envious or boastful or arrogant or rude. It does not insist on its own way; it is not irritable or resentful; it does not rejoice in wrongdoing, but rejoices in the truth. It bears all things, believes all things, hopes all things, endures all things. Love never ends..." (1 Cor 13:4–8);

- becoming ambassadors of reconciliation: "So if anyone is in Christ, there is a new creation: everything old has passed away; see, everything has become new! All this is from God, who reconciled us to himself through Christ, and has given us the ministry of reconciliation" (2 Cor 5:17–18);

- witnessing to our Catholic faith in every area of life;

- persevering in the formation of a Catholic conscience.

While this is certainly not an exhaustive list of activities, they serve as a starting point for reflection as we consider our progress along the path to holiness.

Questions for Reflection & Discussion

1. What is holiness? What would a life intentionally striving for holiness look like in action?

2. Mother Teresa said, "It is not necessary to do great things for God; just do small things with great love." How could this profound instruction help me on my journey toward holiness?

3. What am I doing specifically and intentionally to make progress on my personal journey to holiness? What three specific behaviors will I incorporate into my daily life to help me become more Christlike? (Is 11:1–2; Gal 5:22–23; 1 Cor 13:4–8)

4. The communal call to holiness includes encouraging, supporting, and at times challenging others on their journey of

faith. In what specific ways do I do this? When have I recently received another's challenge regarding my behaviors, attitudes, and so on? Did I receive this challenge with openness and gratitude or with defensiveness and anger?

5. In what ways could I improve in these areas?

Prayer & Reflection

Called to be disciples,
 we come before your throne;
Broken, hurt, and sinful,
 we know we are not alone.

Help us in our struggle,
 Lord, help us in our call
So we may be ambassadors
 who bring your light to all.

Notes

_____

_____

_____

_____

_____

2

Understanding Conflict

How many conflicts do you experience during a typical day? Before you say "None," think about the many times you face difficult or stressful situations: the slow-moving vehicle that won't let you pass; the sales clerk who ignores you when you clearly have a question; the weather that turns suddenly cold and wet when you had planned an outing.

A twenty-four-hour day gives us countless opportunities to respond to stressful situations. Although this book focuses on interpersonal conflict, even our internal conflicts affect us each day. Sometimes we're feeling the conflict of the day as soon as our eyes open in the morning! We are worried or anxious about what we need to do or where we need to go, or (especially) with whom we have to interact.

In this session, we'll explore our understanding of what conflict is and consider some of its causes.

Let's [define] conflict as a difference in opinion or purpose that frustrates someone's goals or desires. This definition is broad enough to include innocuous variations in taste, such as one spouse wanting to vacation in the mountains while the other prefers the waterfront, as well as hostile arguments, such as

> • What is your immediate and emotional reaction to the word "conflict"? Don't think about the word, simply react to it. What feelings does the word evoke?
>
> • Where an intellectual response may acknowledge the positive opportunities in conflict, most, if not all, of our emotional reactions are negative, such as fear, anger, fighting, war, battle, argument, and so on.

fights, quarrels, lawsuits, or church divisions. (Sande, 29–30)

Consider the two parts of this definition. The first part—a difference in opinion or purpose—points out that conflict is rooted in differences, but the second part explains that a difference only becomes a conflict when it frustrates another's goals or desires. So differences can exist without causing conflict, but when my different opinion or purpose gets in your way, our conflict is set in motion!

Should we be surprised by conflict? In a fallen world, conflict is inevitable and should be expected (see Rom 3:10–18; Jas 4:1–3; Acts 15:1–2, 36–39). "Sin is present in human history; any attempt to ignore it or to give this dark reality other names would be futile." (CCC, 386) Is conflict good or bad? The Church does not teach that all conflict is bad; instead, it teaches that some differences are natural and beneficial. Since God has created us as unique individuals, Catholics will often have different opinions, convictions, desires, perspectives, and priorities. Remember, we are "many parts in one body" (1 Cor 12:12–13).

Many of these differences are not inherently right or wrong; they are simply the result of God-given diversity and personal preferences. When handled properly, disagreements in these areas can stimulate productive dialogue, encourage creativity, promote helpful change, and generally make life more interesting. Therefore, although we should seek unity in our relationships, we should not demand uniformity (see Eph 4:1–13).

Not all conflict is neutral or beneficial, however. The Church teaches that many disagreements are the direct result of sinful motives and behavior.

Without the knowledge of the Revelation of God we cannot recognize sin clearly and are tempted to explain it as merely a developmental flaw, a psychological weakness, a mistake, or the necessary consequence of an inadequate social structure, etc. Only in the knowledge of God's plan for man can we grasp that sin is an abuse of the freedom of loving him and loving one another. (CCC, 387)

Most importantly, the Church teaches that we should see conflict neither as an inconvenience nor as an occasion for selfish gain, but rather as an opportunity to demonstrate the presence and power of God. It is a test for us: do we express with our lives the faith we profess with our mouths? Do we "walk our talk?"

Impelled by divine charity, they do good to all men especially to those of the household of the faith (cf. Gal. 6:10), laying aside "all malice and all deceit and pretense, and envy, and all slander" (1 Pet 2:1), and thereby they draw men to Christ. (*Apostolicam Actuositatem*, 4)

Can't we still hear the counsel of the nuns in parochial school when things went wrong? "Offer it up!" may still be sage advice for us, even today!

Conflicts: Where Do They Come From?

Those conflicts and disputes among you, where do they come from? Do they not come from your cravings that are at war within you? You want something and do not have it; so you commit murder. And you covet something and cannot obtain it; so you engage in disputes and conflicts. You do not have, because you do not ask. You ask and do not receive, because you ask wrongly, in order to spend what you get on your pleasures. (Jas 4:1–3)

While we often think we can identify the causes of the conflicts in our lives, the Word of God points us to a deeper and more fundamental reality: original sin. We are preoccupied with our own passions, and this innate and interior brokenness expresses itself in our interpersonal relationships, frequently in painful and destructive ways. How does our sinfulness cause conflict?

- *Misunderstandings.* Our sinfulness limits our perceptions; we see things through our limited filters, and we speculate, draw conclusions, and leap to judgments that are frequently in error (cf. Acts 15:22–29).

- *Differences in values, goals, gifts, calling, priorities, expectations, interests, or opinions.* Scripture tells us there are many parts, but the same body. God values all of us: male and female, young and old, disabled and physically whole, Hispanic and Asian, all with unique perspectives and perceptions. All have their contribution to make (cf. 1 Cor 12:12–31).

- *Competition over limited resources* (cf. Gen 13:1–12). From three family members sharing a single bathroom to parishes suffering from the shortage of priests, human and fiscal resources, our belief is that we must see to our own needs or be left wanting.

- *Sinful attitudes and desires that lead to sinful words and actions* (cf. Jas 4:1–3, CCC 386–409). "Man set himself against God and sought to attain his goal apart from God…Therefore man is split within himself. As a result, all of human life, whether individual or collective, shows itself to be a dramatic struggle between good and evil, between light and darkness" (*Gaudium et Spes*, 13).

The parable of the prodigal son identifies the elder son's self-righteousness as the sinful passion that keeps him from being able to embrace and forgive his brother and father. Our own sinful passions are often more subtle and frequently take the form of imposing expectations upon others, which is another common source of interpersonal conflict in our lives.

Scott McKenzie of Cargill Associates illustrates the process we experience when our expectations are broken. In his diagram, we see that before we commit to someone or something, we explore possibilities and develop expectations. This exploration is what leads us to make our initial commitment. What follows is a period of great excitement, creativity, energy, and productivity. This is a period of high enthusiasm and great optimism—the traditional "honeymoon" phase of any project or relationship.

Invariably, however, before long we become disappointed and frustrated when reality falls short of our expectations. This is where we realize that the new job isn't quite what we'd hoped it to be, the person with whom we are in relationship actually has flaws, and our children are really not rocket scientists. We enter the wilderness where we are more resigned than committed, opening the doors for sabotage, withdrawal, stalemate, and even depression. We become angry and we blame others for our predicament. Unless we face

Dealing with Broken Expectations & Change
Scott McKenzie, Cargill and Associates

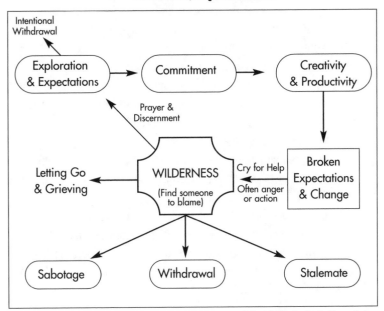

© Scott McKenzie. Used with permission.

reality, let go, and grieve our prior expectations, we can remain in this desolation indefinitely.

The path to new exploration and possible recommitment requires that we take time for prayer and discernment. Our prayer may call us to intentional withdrawal to move in a new direction, as in an occupational change, or it may result in a renewal of our

Our sinfulness manifests itself in our interpersonal relationships, frequently causing pain and devastation. The parable of the prodigal son (Lk 15:11–32) is a study of this dynamic.

This parable is often used as an instruction on the merciful and forgiving love of our heavenly Father. At the same time, it calls us to reflect on how our own attitudes and behaviors are mirrored by the brothers. While we may readily relate to the wastefulness and remorse of the younger son, we resist admitting that we, too, can be as judgmental and unforgiving as the elder son. We see jealousy and resentment toward his brother and toward the mercy of his father. In fact, his very language embodies disdain, critical judgment, and lack of forgiveness as he rejects his relationship with his brother with the words, "that son of yours."

The father strives to bring him back to love and mercy with the words, "your brother." If we are truly honest with ourselves, we may admit to sharing more of the older brother's feelings and thoughts than we would initially wish to acknowledge. Who of us has not sat in judgment and condemnation of another? Who has not held back forgiveness for the hurts and offenses we've suffered? In these situations, the words from the Gospel of Matthew haunt us as they stress that relational reconciliation is an integral component our worship of God:

"So then, if you are bringing your offering to the altar and there remember that your brother has something against you, leave your offering there before the altar, go and be reconciled with your brother first, and then come back and present your offering" (Matt 5:23–24).

original commitment. The intentional withdrawal born of prayerful discernment differs from reactive withdrawal in the wilderness, which is instead rooted in emotionalism. Knowing how to move through the cycle reduces the possibility for conflict.

Another cause of conflict is when we make assumptions and judgments about others' intentions and behaviors. How often do we leap to judgment without consciously thinking through what we are observing and how we are interpreting it?

We frequently find ourselves in error when we draw conclusions without validating our assumptions. For example, what does it mean when we pass our neighbors and they ignore our greeting? Do we sometimes jump to the conclusion that they don't like us or that they are angry with us for some reason? The possibility that there may be other reasons for their apparent slight never occurs to us.

Having come to our conclusion, we may decide to ignore them or speak ill of them. Now they are left to make their own assumptions about our behavior, thus planting the seeds of interpersonal conflict, which frequently come to full bloom in a very short time (Sande, 243).

Questions for Reflection & Discussion

1. Think of a recent conflict and ask yourself: What caused it? Can I identify any sin involved—especially my own? (It is usually more natural and even more comfortable to point out another's sins and failings rather than our own!)

2. Read Romans 7:14–25. How is this struggle manifested in my own life?

3. In what ways have I failed in my stewardship of goods and relationships that God has given me? In what ways have I been wasteful, wanton, or willful, like the younger son in the parable of the prodigal son?

4. When have I behaved like the elder son in the parable of the prodigal son, sitting in judgment and condemnation of another? When have I held back forgiveness for the hurts and offenses I've suffered?

5. When have I been so moved by God's grace that, like the father in the parable of the prodigal son, I was eager to forgive another even before they expressed remorse?

6. Read Matthew 5:23–24: Why is relational reconciliation an important component of our worship of God? What specific behaviors do I have to change to respond to God's will for me in conflict?

7. Take time to reflect on the Broken Expectations diagram, recalling examples in your own life of moving through the cycle of broken expectations. These examples may include jobs, marriage, education, friendships, church experiences, and so on. If you are in a group, share your experiences.

8. Can I recall a specific incident when I made assumptions and judgments that later proved to be false? Share with the group, if appropriate.

Prayer & Reflection

We know we get into conflict, Lord,
    we cause it by our sin.
Yet in weakness we hold fast
    to the hurtful state we're in.

Confused, bewildered by the foe
    we stumble in our pride.
Help us, Lord, to know your voice;
    keep us by your side.

Since turmoil we will always know
    until we see your face,
We ask your presence in our hearts
    with the gift of your sweet grace.

Notes

_____

_____

_____

_____

_____

_____

_____

_____

_____

_____

_____

_____

_____

_____

_____

_____

_____

_____

_____

_____

3

Responding to Conflict

There are three basic ways that people respond to conflict. These responses may be arranged on a curve that resembles a hill. On the left slope of the hill we find the escape responses to conflict. On the right side are the attack responses. And in the center we find the peacemaking responses.

Imagine that this hill is covered with ice. If you go too far to the left or the right, you can lose your footing and slide down the slope. Similarly, when you experience conflict, it is easy to become defensive or antagonistic. Both responses make matters worse and can lead to more extreme reactions.

If you want to stay on top of this slippery slope, you need to do two things. First, ask God to help you resist the natural inclination to escape or attack when faced with conflict. Second, ask God to help you develop the ability to live out the gospel by using the peacemaking response that is best suited to resolving a particular conflict. Let's look at each of these responses in more detail (Sande, 22–23).

The Slippery Slope:
A Spectrum of Responses to Conflict

Escape responses

The three responses found on the left side of the curve are directed at getting away from conflict situations rather than resolving them. While we may use these means to make it appear as if conflict does not exist, we are simply employing a peace *faking* response to conflict.

- *Denial.* Pretending that a conflict does not exist, blaming the other person instead of taking responsibility for our own role, or refusing to do what we should do to resolve the conflict properly are all forms of denial. These responses will never result in a true resolution to the situation.

- *Flight.* Fleeing from the situation or the person with whom we are having a conflict serves only to delay addressing the matter and can result in making the conflict more difficult to resolve. We can flee physically by avoiding others or emotionally by withdrawing our attentiveness from the relationship. Flight can be a legitimate response when there is a danger of harm present (see 1 Sam 19:9–10). Removing ourselves temporarily from the heat of a conflict—which can look like flight—is an effective strategy when a "time out" is needed. We may do this in order to allow emotions to abate or to take time to pray about what is happening, and set a time to get back together to work things out.

- *Suicide.* Killing oneself is the ultimate escape response; the decision made by those who believe they have run out of alternatives. Tragically, our country is presently ranked second in the world in teenage suicides; a reality that we must address individually, as a Church, as a community, and as a nation.

Attack responses

The three responses found on the right side of the slope are directed at bringing as much pressure to bear on opponents as is necessary to defeat their claims and eliminate their opposition. These attack responses are assault, litigation, and murder. It is obvious that none of these responses brings about peace or reconciliation.

- *Assault.* Using force or intimidation (physical, verbal, financial, or otherwise) to compel an opponent to give in to our demands is the tool of a bully. Brute force is not uncommon in childhood, but while most of us believe that we have grown out of this response—and no one wants to be considered a bully—many of us have participated in the most common types of assault against others: gossip, triangulation, labeling, and name-calling. Disparaging remarks made about others behind their backs may seem innocuous, but a great many conflicts have their roots in this meanness. These reflect a deceitfulness and cowardice that spreads conflicts and makes them more difficult to reconcile.

- *Litigation.* Taking our adversaries to court is too often our society's first response to conflict. Rather than being willing to work things out with another, we assign our conflict to lawyers and pay them to fight it out on our behalf. It seems to have become the adult counterpart to children lashing out at their playmates in the sandbox. Court dockets are overburdened with every manner of dispute. In "Procedures for Resolving Conflict" (USCCB), the Catholic bishops admonish us to resolve disputes by practicing conciliation techniques rather than automatically asserting legal rights (59). While there may be some legitimate uses for litigation, it should be engaged in as a last resort, after exhausting all "work-it-out" responses.

- *Murder.* Killing a person who opposes you is certainly not an option for anyone striving to put flesh on the gospel of Jesus Christ. Murder is always wrong. Yet many people feel justified in a more common type of "murder"—killing the reputations of others through malicious speech.

Peacemaking Responses

The six responses found along the top portion of the slope are directed at finding a just and mutually agreeable solution to a conflict. They are the peacemaking—or "work-it-out"—responses. If we are to avoid the Escape Responses, which embody "peace faking," and the Attack Responses, which are "peace breaking," we can follow the Peacemaking Responses. These responses may be divided into two categories: personal and assisted.

Personal peacemaking responses involve only the parties in dispute and they include overlooking, reconciling, and negotiating. However, there are times when the assistance of others is needed to bring about a positive outcome to a dispute. Assisted responses can range from informal consultation to formal intervention by family members, neighbors, professionals, parishioners, or clergy and other Church leaders, and they include mediation, arbitration, and accountability (Mt 18:16–17).

Assisting others who are embroiled in conflict presents an excellent opportunity to witness to our faith and support them in their journey toward holiness. It should be noted here that seeking aid from others during a conflict is not the same as lobbying others through gossip and triangulation to support our position.

- *Overlook an offense.* When a relationship is not substantially broken by the wrong that was done, giving the benefit of the doubt and the gift of forgiveness to the other by overlooking the matter follows the spirit of Proverbs 19:11: "Those with good sense are slow to anger, and it is their glory to overlook an offense." In our humanness, we all make mistakes that have the potential of offending others. Depending upon the severity of the offense, it may be appropriately resolved by simply forgetting the matter and moving on. Note that overlooking the offense is different than denying it because it is not an effort at ignoring the problem; rather, it first acknowledges that the wrong was committed and then freely makes the choice to forgive.

- *Conciliation.* This response involves talking over our personal differences with the other, with the goal of achieving personal forgiveness and reconciliation. If we are willing to put aside defensiveness and become vulnerable for the sake of the relationship, we are recognizing that the relationship is of greater importance to God than the issue that divided us in the first place. Matthew 18:15 directs us to "win back" the other through honest dialogue.

- *Negotiation.* Resolving substantive issues through a bargaining process (where we seek a mutually agreeable settlement of our differences through an exchange of promises) again ensures that we have put the relationship above self-interest. St. Paul instructs us: "Let each of you look not to your own interests, but to the interests of others" (Phil 2:4). Conflicts that involve substantive issues, such as time, money, property, etc., are resolved fairly with this approach, which usually requires compromise on the part of each person.

- *Mediation.* Consulting a mutually respected third party can improve communication and help facilitate a resolution. Mediators help the disputing parties discover areas of agreement or commonality and sometimes challenge them to see things differently. The mediator, as a neutral party, is merely a facilitator; the final agreement is worked out by the parties themselves. This makes mediation particularly attractive when other attempts to reconcile have failed. Mediation can be very formal (hiring a professional mediator) or rather informal (asking a friend to listen to both sides and make helpful observations).

- *Arbitration.* Taking the dispute before a "judge" to render a decision may be necessary if other attempts have been unsuccessful. An arbitrator's decisions are binding upon both parties, and can be documented in public records. In this response, the parties relinquish control of the outcome. This may be less satisfying than if they had come to a voluntary agreement through mediation.

- *Accountability.* Submitting a dispute to the authority of the Church for resolution is the final assisted peacemaking response to conflict. This response is not widespread in the Catholic Church today since leaders are generally not trained to apply Church teaching, Scripture, and canon law to settle disputes among its members. Accountability to the Church and to one's faith was, however, a strong element in the early Church, as the writings of Paul testify. This concept was a source of the Church's Code of Canon Law, which has, in recent years, been virtually confined to marriage cases. The teaching of Jesus in Matthew 18:17, however, could prompt us to reconsider the role of the Church in restoring peace: "If the member refuses to listen to them, tell it to the church."

The spirit of Catholic conciliation calls us to be humble and consider the questions, "Have I considered this issue from all perspectives?" and "Are there places of agreement that I have not acknowl-edged?" as well as "What's really important here?" and "Has my behavior in this matter been hurtful or sinful?"

Catholics can stay on top of conflict by depending on God's love and grace and by faithfully following his commands. Our faith calls us to a counter-cultural response to much of what the world values and promotes, as the saints have modeled for us in their own lives. What better opportunities exist for outwardly displaying the faith we profess than the conflicts that invariably arise in our life?

Questions for Reflection & Discussion

1. What is my usual response to conflict? Why do I react this way? How effective has this response been in resolving con-flict?

2. What types of conflict resolution were modeled to me dur-ing my childhood? During my adolescence? Were they effec-tive means of resolving conflict?

3. How are most of the conflicts in which I find myself resolved?

4. What escape response (pages 22-23) do I tend to use most?

5. What is the attack response (pages 23-24) I tend to use the most?

6. What is the peacemaking response (pages 25-26) I tend to use most?

7. Which of the peacemaking responses do I avoid using? Why?

8. Read the following Scripture passages, then identify the response to conflict presented in the passage.

   1 Samuel 19:9–12 (David's response to Saul's attempts to kill him): mediation? flight? murder?

   Acts 6:1–7 (the apostles' response to the conflict about dis-

tributing food): denial? overlook? arbitration?
Matthew 12:15–22 (the Pharisees' response to Jesus): assault?
negotiation? suicide?

Prayer & Reflection

We need your grace and strength, O Lord,
    to stay upon the slope.
Left to ourselves we slip and slide;
    we stumble, fall, and grope.

It is your will we seek to learn
    relinquishing our rights.
For who among us has no fault
    in our conflicts and our fights?

We come before you with our prayer,
    humble, forlorn, and frail;
For it is only by your grace and love
    our step will never fail.

Notes

_____

_____

_____

_____

_____

_____

_____

_____

_____

_____

_____

_____

_____

_____

_____

4

Step One: Glorify God

We know we are called by God to witness to our faith in all areas of our lives. Oftentimes, the way we are to conduct ourselves is clear as we follow the general precepts of moral and ethical living.

Many times, however, the specific way we enflesh our discipleship is not as obvious. This is certainly true when we find ourselves in conflict. Does God want us to become doormats and allow others to walk all over us? (No!) As Christians, when do we stand our ground against another? What does Christian discipleship look like in the practical struggles of life?

Scripture and Church teaching support a sequential, four-step approach to dealing with conflict. These four steps, also called the "Four Gs," put our Catholic faith and our personal relationship with God first in all things, but especially when we're challenged by conflict.

It is too easy to fall into the trap modeled by the world, which

> The highest perfection consists not in interior favors, or in great raptures or in visions, or in the spirit of prophecy, but in bringing our wills so closely in conformity with the will of God that, as soon as we realize He wills something, we desire it for ourselves with all our might, and take the bitter with the sweet.
>
> —St. Teresa of Avila

is to approach conflict with an attitude of rights and entitlements. Hold your ground, fight for your rights, and win at all costs are themes we see repeated constantly on the street, in the news, the workplace, the books we read, the music we hear, and the movies we watch.

Our society abhors weakness, and it seems to view peaceful means of resolving conflict as weak. For a country that was founded on a deep faith in God, we seem to have abandoned the tendency to follow his guidance when life's pressures become too great. Remembering our call to holiness when faced with conflict, however, can be the critical step to restoring true peace and reconciliation with others.

God's Will First

Imagine how different the world would be if all Catholics stopped to glorify God when disputes arose among us! Asking ourselves the question, "How can I please and honor God in this situation?" when we are offended by another is a radical example of truly living our faith. This means that we are to place our trust in God, who sees a much bigger picture than we do, and not in our own selfish desire to be vindicated when wronged.

Scripture reminds us where we are to focus our thoughts:

So if you have been raised with Christ, seek the things that are above, where Christ is, seated at the right hand of God. Set your minds on things that are above, not on things that are on earth... (Col 3:1–2).

This helps us to remember that the power of spreading peace in the world comes from the strength and grace God provides us through Jesus. "We have this treasure in clay jars, so that it may be made clear that this extraordinary power belongs to God and does not come from us" (2 Cor 4:7). Scripture abounds with examples of people like us who turn to God during times of conflict, as found in Psalm 109:26 and Matthew 15:25.

The cycle that Jesus himself followed of withdraw, pray, and act (WPA) models for us the discipline of stepping aside to prayerfully seek God's will when discerning the response to conflict that will most build relationships. When conflict seems to demand an immediate reaction, we can take a moment to re-establish our perspective and center ourselves in faith through the WPA response.

This counter-cultural response of giving glory to God as soon as we realize we are in conflict means that we are actively and consciously surrendering our will to the will of God. The sacrament of Eucharist, which is the "source and summit" of our Catholic faith (*Lumen Gentium*, 11), is a physical manifestation of this attitudinal surrender to God's dominion in our lives. We humbly approach the Body and Blood of our Lord to be strengthened as Christ's disciples. The Eucharist is both the "sign and sublime cause" (CCC, 1325) of this union with Christ, which enables us to sacrifice our very selves as Jesus did.

Have you ever thought of the ways that we sacrifice our own wills in a typical day? We stand in the fog and rain watching our children's sporting events when we'd rather be home, warm and dry. We take time to listen to a co-worker's struggles when projects and deadlines are pressing in upon us. We give up our right-of-way in traffic when we, too, are in a hurry. These are just small, everyday examples of the way we mirror the great sacrifice of Christ upon the cross and give praise to our heavenly Father. Doing so transforms our verbal prayer into genuine acts of praise.

> Every joy and suffering, every event and need can become the matter for thanksgiving which, sharing in that of Christ, should fill one's whole life: "Give thanks in all circumstances."
>
> —1 Thess 5:18 ; CCC, 2648

Praise is the form of prayer which recognizes most immediately that God is God. It lauds God for his own sake and gives him glory, quite beyond what he does, but simply because HE IS... (CCC, 2639).

Conflict as Opportunity

Prayer at the moment of conflict gets our priorities straight. It is a radical notion, perhaps, but one that honors and reflects our striving toward holiness, and renders our hearts more open to true reconciliation. Therefore, instead of simply being a dismal situation, conflict actually provides us with three particular opportunities to grow in our faith.

Those who recall the lessons in the *Baltimore Catechism* will remember reading that God made us "to know him, to love him, and to serve him in this world, and to be happy with him forever in heaven" (Question 2, Book 1). We can use this teaching to find three opportunities that motivate our efforts at resolution, present in every conflict; that is, to know, love, and serve God.

- *To know God.* God is unfathomable and mysterious; we come to know him only by the gift of his grace. Grace comes to us through many different channels, chief among them are the seven sacraments. These sacraments reflect our journey of faith that takes us from baptism, our entrance into the Church, to our final anointing, when we are preparing to join God in paradise. It is grace that opens our minds and hearts to the witness of Christ who reveals the Father to us. Striving to know God's will for us in conflict situations will ensure that our responses are pleasing to God.

- *To love God.* God calls us into a close intimate relationship, and asks us to make him a priority in our lives. This is not a value in our culture, which attempts to convince us to embrace other priorities. "He who dies with the most toys wins" is the anthem of a culture that focuses our attentions on excessive consumption and instant gratification. When we create idols in our life, such as things, philosophies, habits, and relationships that interfere with our relationship with God, we lose sight of who we are as God's beloved sons and daughters. "We know that all things work together for good for those who love God, who are called according to his purpose" (Rom 8:28). This awareness changes the way we approach conflict. We love and trust God in even the most difficult situations.

- *To serve God.* As we grow in knowledge and love of God, we desire more and more to serve him. Serving God means serving others by being his hands, eyes, ears, and mouth in the world. It means being the living answer to the question, "What would love do?" This attitude of service determines the way we respond in conflict.

Jesus Christ is the model for how to know, love, and serve the Father. As we are formed more and more into his image, we draw closer and closer to God. We then see all things in new ways.

Questions for Reflection & Discussion

1. How do I try to conform my will to the will of God?

2. In what specific ways do I demonstrate my trust of God in difficult times?

3. How do my relationships mirror the Trinitarian unity that Jesus speaks of in Jn. 17:21–22 in the area of service to others? In what ways could my relationships be improved to better reflect this Godly unity?

4. In what specific ways is my life "conformed to Christ"? In what areas do I still need God's grace to strengthen my will? How am I working intentionally in these areas?

5. Recall instances where you have been successful in praising God in the midst of turmoil or difficulty.

Prayer & Reflection

Each time we face a conflict,
>we seek to praise the Lord.
What a strange, unworldly answer
>to our secular discord!

Of course we are his witnesses,
>embodying here on earth
The wisdom of his counsel,
>and the purpose of his birth.

So help us as we serve you
>and assist us all our life,
As we face each new dispute
>with grace amid the strife.

Notes

_____

_____

_____

_____

_____

_____

5

Step Two: Get the Log Out of Your Own Eye

Jesus said, "Do not judge, so that you may not be judged. For with the judgment you make you will be judged, and the measure you give will be the measure you get. Why do you see the speck in your neighbor's eye, but do not notice the log in your own eye?...first take the log out of your own eye, and then you will see clearly to take the speck out of your neighbor's eye. (Mt 7:1–5)

We know that our faith is a counter-cultural journey. Experience tells us that the values of our Western culture are contrary to our gospel call. It should come as no surprise, then, that the second step of the Catholic conciliation process, get the log out of your own eye, is as radical as the first.

Once we have rooted ourselves in prayer and praise of God, we take responsibility for our own actions, for our own role in the conflict. This is contrary to our natural tendency to shift the blame in a conflict to the other.

The contrast is clear: our culture says, "Find someone to blame," but our faith tells us, "Look within and acknowledge your own fault in the matter." If we acknowledge the reality of original sin and our own innate woundedness, we are more inclined to self-reflection than to blaming others. And this self-reflection helps to get us in touch with God's will in the conflict.

"The Gospel is the revelation in Jesus Christ of God's mercy to sinners....The same is true of the Eucharist, the sacrament of redemption: 'This is my blood of the covenant, which is poured out for many for the forgiveness of sins'" (CCC, 1846; Lk 15, Mt 1:21, Mt 26:28). We even begin our liturgical worship acknowledging our sins in the Penitential Rite.

> It is important for every person to be sufficiently present to himself in order to hear and follow the voice of his conscience. This requirement of interiority is all the more necessary as life often distracts us from any reflection, self-examination or introspection. (As St. Augustine encourages us,) "Return to your conscience, question it....Turn inward and in everything you do, see God as your witness." (CCC, 1779)

To receive God's mercy, we must recognize and acknowledge our sins. "If we say we have no sin, we deceive ourselves, and the truth is not in us. If we confess our sins, he is faithful and just, and will forgive our sins and cleanse us from all unrighteousness" (CCC, 1847; 1 Jn 8–9). What is sin?

> Sin is an offense against reason, truth, and right conscience; it is failure in genuine love for God and neighbor...It has been defined as "an utterance, a deed, or a desire contrary to the eternal law."...Sin is an offense against God: "Against you, you alone, have I sinned, and done that which is evil in your sight" (Ps 51:4). Sin sets itself against God's love for us and turns our hearts away from it." (CCC, 1849–1850)

So, when we sin against our neighbor in our thoughts, words, or actions, we sin against God as well.

Our Catholic faith encourages us to develop the habit of doing an examen, which, according to the Catholic Encyclopedia, is "an examination of conscience made daily or at special intervals as a devotional practice (not by necessity as before the Sacrament of Reconciliation)." When we find ourselves in conflict, we can intentionally direct this examen toward discovering the "logs" in our own eyes, as this second step in the process directs us to do.

There are three types of "logs" that we can identify as we reflect on our own role in any given conflict. The first "log" is our attitudes. What types of attitudes might bring us into conflict with others, or at least contribute to a conflict? Have we been overly critical, negative, judgmental, self-righteous, proud, or disdainful? If so, we could reflect upon Philippians 4:8:

> Finally, beloved, whatever is true, whatever is honorable, whatever is just, whatever is pure, whatever is pleasing, whatever is commendable, if there is any excellence and if there is anything worthy of praise, think about these things.

This is what we should focus upon: our attitudes should be ones of hope, trust, love, and humility. Usually, when we are enmeshed in conflict, these are not our dispositions. So as we look for ways that we have contributed to a conflict, we could conduct an "attitude inventory," and get in touch with this sinful "log."

I confess to Almighty God, and to you my brothers and sisters, that I have sinned through my own fault, in my thoughts and in my words, in what I have done and in what I have failed to do. And I ask blessed Mary, ever virgin, all the angels and saints, and you, my brothers and sisters, to pray for me to the Lord our God. May almighty God have mercy on us, forgive us our sins, and bring us to everlasting life. Amen.

Another "log" we could reflect upon is our sinful words or actions. Have we been gossiping about others? Have we reacted with hurtful, angry words toward others? Have we appeared contrite and repentant while we have actually been self-serving? Have we lied or subtly misrepresented the truth? As Scripture tells us, "Let no evil talk come out of your mouths, but only what is useful for building up, as there is need, so that your words may give grace to those who hear" (Eph 4:29). If we follow this instruction, God's will, and not our own, will be done.

A third "log" is sins of omission. (How many of you just had a nostalgic moment?) These refer to those instances when we know what God is asking of us, but we fail to do it. We may fail to respond in these situations for several reasons: it may be inconvenient, we may not think that we have the time, we may not be sure how our effort would be received, or we may be just plain selfish. Again, Scripture is clear: "Anyone, then, who knows the right thing to do and fails to do it, commits sin" (Jas 4:17).

During our daily examen, we are essentially asking ourselves a critical question, "Have I again put my own will before God's will in any and all situations in my day?" When we find ourselves in conflict, we often lose sight of our call to holiness and cling to our own sinful will. Developing the discipline where we pause during the day to identify our "logs"—even when we are not in conflict—will serve us well when conflict does rage in our lives. Without this discipline, we tend to revert to our human weakness of pointing a finger at others while justifying our own thoughts, words, and actions.

Not only is identifying our "logs" good for self-reflection as we journey toward holiness, we can also use the practice to begin resolving conflict by being willing to go to the other and admit our fault. There are some important elements we should include as we go to another to admit our own contribution to the conflict.

Acknowledging Our Fault

There are specific elements of an acknowledgment of our own fault in a conflict situation that, if we use them, will help the other person to hear better what we have to say and to be more open to God's grace. These elements, which we refer to as the "seven As" of acknowledging our sin (Sande, 126–134), call us to:

- *Address everyone involved.* Those drawn into the conflict through gossip, triangulation, or sinful words and actions need to be addressed in our repentance. This includes God, to whom we go in the sacrament of reconciliation.

- *Avoid if, but, and maybe.* These words excuse our responsibility, discount the other person's pain, and protect us by keeping us in the realms of generality and vagueness. We need to be clear and precise about our sin.

- *Admit specifically.* Focus on all attitudes, words, and actions that have contributed to the conflict.

- *Acknowledge the hurt.* We need to express sincere sorrow for the pain we've caused.

- *Accept the consequences.* We should realize that we are not finished after we make an apology; relationship re-building takes work and sometimes other types of restitution are necessary.

- *Alter your behavior.* Most people, when asked how they know others are sincere in their repentance, point to a change in future behavior as the best evidence of their sincerity.

- *Ask for forgiveness.* We humbly ask the other for forgiveness, with no demands, expectations, or deadlines.

When we fail to recognize and acknowledge our own sin, we are like a proud and haughty person striding boldly and proudly through life—in a hospital gown with the back undone! Often, we even try to stand before God in that pompous posture. On the other hand, God tells us, "If my people who are called by my name humble themselves, pray, seek my face, and turn from their wicked ways, then I will hear from heaven, and will forgive their sin…" (2 Chr 7:14). So our way is clear.

> The confession (or disclosure) of sins, even from a simply human point of view, frees us and facilitates our reconciliation with others. Through such an admission man looks squarely at the sins he is guilty of, takes responsibility for them, and thereby opens himself again to God and to the communion of the Church in order to make a new future possible. (CCC, 1455)

Our willingness to be humble and vulnerable in front of the other will oftentimes break down more walls that stand between us than any other single response we could make.

As we practice getting the logs out of our own eyes, we should remember the words of Jesus, "For I tell you, unless your righteousness exceeds that of the scribes and Pharisees, you will never enter the kingdom of heaven" (Mt 5:20). It's important that we reflect on our sinfulness as it shows itself in our contribution to the conflict, understanding that true repentance is more than just a feeling. True repentance is rooted in humility.

> O my God, I am heartily sorry for having offended Thee, and I detest all my sins because of Thy just punishments, but most of all because they offend Thee, my God, Who art all-good and deserving of all my love. I firmly resolve, with the help of Thy grace, to sin no more and to avoid the near occasions of sin. Amen.

By definition, repentance is sorrow or contrition for one's sins. True repentance includes a conversion of heart, a turning or returning to God. It is interior, but it is also manifested through our acts of repentance that come with the granting of grace by God.

In this regard, four elements of genuine repentance are self-examination, confession, restitution, and change (Sande, 118, 131). As we read in Scripture: "Repent and turn to God and do deeds consistent with repentance" (Acts 26:20), and "Bear fruit worthy of repentance" (Mt 3:8).

Questions for Reflection & Discussion

1. What value, if any, do I see in practicing a regular examination of conscience?

2. Which of the "logs" (pages 30-31) are ones that I see as part of my sinfulness? What "logs" may be the most difficult for me to uncover personally?

3. What advantages do I see in looking specifically at my own culpability in a conflict?

4. Which of the "seven As" are easy for me to do? Which of the "seven As" are most difficult for me?

7. What has been my experience of going to someone, admitting my sin, and asking for forgiveness? If it was negative, does this experience create an obstacle for me as I think about doing this in the future?

8. After reading the Litany of Humility that follows, what parts of the prayer evoke a particular response in me, and why?

The Litany of Humility

O Jesus, meek and humble of heart, hear me.

From the desire of being esteemed,
　　deliver me O Jesus.
From the desire of being loved,
　　deliver me O Jesus.
From the desire of being extolled,
　　deliver me O Jesus.
From the desire of being honored,
　　deliver me O Jesus.
From the desire of being praised,
　　deliver me O Jesus.
From the desire of being preferred to others,
　　deliver me O Jesus.
From the desire of being consulted,
　　deliver me O Jesus.
From the desire of being approved,
　　deliver me O Jesus.

From the fear of being humiliated,
  deliver me O Jesus.
From the fear of being despised,
  deliver me O Jesus.
From the fear of being rebuked,
  deliver me O Jesus.
From the fear of being calumniated,
  deliver me O Jesus.
From the fear of being forgotten,
  deliver me O Jesus.
From the fear of being ridiculed,
  deliver me O Jesus.
From the fear of being wronged,
  deliver me O Jesus.
From the fear of being suspected,
  deliver me O Jesus.

That others may be loved more than I,
  Jesus, grant me the grace to desire it.
That others may be esteemed more than I,
  Jesus, grant me the grace to desire it.
That in the opinion of the world, others may increase, and I may decrease,
  Jesus, grant me the grace to desire it.
That others may be chosen and I set aside,
  Jesus, grant me the grace to desire it.
That others may be praised and I unnoticed,
  Jesus, grant me the grace to desire it.
That others may be preferred to me in everything,
  Jesus, grant me the grace to desire it.
That others may become holier than I,
  provided that I may become as holy as I should,
  Jesus, grant me the grace to desire it.
              —From Letters of Association, Abbey of Gethsemani, KY

Prayer & Reflection

I find myself in conflict, Lord,
    looking for anyone to blame
For my hurt and tears and suffering,
    for my woundedness and pain.

And then your voice becomes so clear
    and I know just what to do,
As you tell me where to start to change;
    you say, "Begin with you."

And the truth that you are sharing
    cuts to the marrow so fine:
The splinter in the other's eye
dwarfs the log that is in mine.

So I look at all my attitudes
    and my thoughts and words as well,
The ones that others have endured
    and the ones I'd never tell.

And I know that I am guilty;
    I'm convicted in my sin.
And your loving voice assures me,
    "Come to me; I'll let you in."

Thank you for your mercy, Lord,
    and thank you for your love,
That keeps my heart and mind and soul
    on the treasure up above.

Notes

_____

_____

_____

_____

_____

_____

_____

_____

_____

_____

_____

_____

_____

_____

6

Step Three: Gently Restore

If another member of the church sins against you, go and point out the fault when the two of you are alone. If the member listens to you, you have regained that one. (Mt 18:15)

When a conflict is too serious to overlook and we've honestly appraised and accepted our role in it, there is a third, crucial step in our journey toward reconciliation: to gently restore. As St. Paul writes in his letter to the Galatians, "My friends, if anyone is detected in a transgression, you who have received the Spirit should restore such a one in a spirit of gentleness" (6:1).

Our culture has conditioned us to blame others as the natural response to conflict and hurtful situations. Blaming others and pointing out their faults—both to their faces and behind their backs—is almost automatic in our society. It has become instinctive for us to focus on the shortcomings of the person with whom we disagree, and look for opportunities to share these opinions and judgments with others. But if we recall God's mercy toward us, we can approach others in a different spirit, a spirit of love rather than condemnation (Sande, 142).

God asks us to put aside our interests and consider the interests of others: "Let each of you look not to your own interests, but to the interests of others" (Phil 2:4). He asks us to build each other up instead of tearing each other down: "Do not let any unwholesome talk come out of your mouths, but only what is helpful for building up others according to their needs that it may benefit those who listen" (Eph 4:29).

God asks us to abandon our need to protect ourselves through defensiveness and stubbornness and replace these with unwavering trust and confidence that he will turn even this conflict into an asset on our journey toward holiness: "We know that all things work together for good for those who love God, who are called according to his purpose" (Rom 8:28).

Confront Others in Love

To confront in love the person with whom we are in conflict requires us to be vulnerable. It means that we become willing to acknowledge our fault and expose the tender place in us that has been hurt. It requires that we relinquish the belief that our position is absolutely right and that our opponent is absolutely wrong.

Confronting the other in love asks us to be humble and to open our hearts to learn more about ourselves and about the other. It recognizes that there is no guarantee that our effort will have the results we desire, but that God asks us to take this risk for the sake of the relationship. Our relationship with the other is more important to God than our pride or our need to be right; in fact, as we have said, it is an integral part of coming to the altar in worship:

So when you are offering your gift at the altar, if you remember that your brother or sister has something against you, leave your gift there before the altar and go; first be reconciled to your brother or sister, and then come and offer your gift. (Mt 5:23)

Not only are we obliged to lovingly confront those with whom we have a dispute, but we must be open to hear from others how our actions and motives have caused pain or harm to them. It's been said that we tend to judge others by their behaviors and ourselves by our intentions. While it may be natural to give ourselves the benefit of the doubt, we must also be willing to extend this benefit to others. Everyone interprets the events of life through the filters of knowledge and past experience. God simply asks that we treat others as gently as we would wish to be treated ourselves.

There are some important and helpful strategies to remember to make this encounter go well.

- *Pray first.* Pray for humility and wisdom before taking action. Prayer should be our first response in every situation, but it is especially critical in conflict situations. To respond as God desires, we must counter not only the human instinct for self-protection but also the influence of our culture to lash out when wronged. Prayer helps us to access divine wisdom.

- *Plan your words carefully.* It is wise to practice what we have to say before we meet with the other person, especially if we tend to become emotional or get off track. It helps to consider how we ourselves would like to be confronted and to choose our words accordingly.

- *Anticipate likely reactions.* How is the other person going to receive our message? Being prepared for several possible responses will keep us focused and sensitive to the other's feelings.

- *Choose the best time and place.* Check with the other to ensure that there is sufficient time to address the situation and identify a place where you'll not be disturbed and you can both feel comfortable.

- *Assume the best about the other until facts prove otherwise.* We generally conjure up everything negative about the people with whom we're in conflict, but if we focus on their positive traits, we'll see them the way God does.

- *Listen carefully.* Ordinarily we spend our "listening time" preparing our response, but if we listen for and acknowledge the other's feelings beneath the words, we'll be demonstrating true care and concern and really hearing what's being said.

- *Speak only to build others up.* Be careful not to attack the other; use language that communicates your message in a positive and productive way.

- *Ask for feedback.* Check for understanding frequently so that your message as well as the one you're receiving is getting through accurately.

- *Recognize limitations.* There may be other obstacles like illness or fatigue that could prevent final resolution at this time, and our own limits may get in the way as well.

It's good to remember that we're not setting out to change others; only God can do that. As we respond differently to conflict in our lives, however, we give others the freedom to respond differently as well—and it is through that change that God's will can emerge (Sande, 162–184).

Whatever the situation might be, we should always show respect for the concerns, traditions, limitations, and special needs of others and ask God to show us how to communicate with them in the way that is most appropriate and helpful to them. (Sande, 147)

Communicate for Success

Utilizing our best communication skills helps us to get our message across most effectively. There are different channels through which we convey our thoughts and feelings. For example, there are the actual words we choose (the linguistic channel); the emphases, rate, pitch, and tone we apply to the words (the para-linguistic channel); and the gestures, expressions, movements, and posture

> Would you rate yourself a good listener? Studies show that adults rate themselves 75% or higher as effective listeners, when in reality most people effectively listen at about a 30% rate. With this in mind, what specific aspect of listening do you need to improve?

that we assume (the nonverbal channel—through which most of the meaning is carried). All these elements combine to affect the message we are trying to communicate.

We should be aware of our personal strengths and weaknesses in communication and work intentionally in each channel to make our message clear and easily understood. For instance, do we express displeasure with the other's message nonverbally before the other person is even finished speaking? This signals that we've reached conclusions and judgments and haven't given the speaker the gift of empathic listening. Do we use sarcasm to drive home our points and in the process diminish others and the perspectives they've shared?

One practice we could strive to follow to improve our communication is called The Lesson of the Three Gates. In this exercise, we pretend to have a giraffe-like neck containing three gates, each with a question on it. Everything we say must pass through these three gates by answering "yes" to the questions.

- The question on the first gate is, "Is it true?" In other words, we agree not to say anything that is not completely truthful. Assuming that what we want to say is, in fact, true, our message proceeds to the second gate.

- The question on the second gate is, "Is it necessary?" To extend this a bit, we can ask, "Does it need to be said?" "Does it need to be said *by me*?" and "Does it need to be said by me *now*?" If we can answer "Yes" to the second gate's questions, we can move to the third gate.

- The question challenging us on the third gate is, "Is it kind?" No matter how difficult the issue may be, our communication can still be considerate of the other. Here we need to be careful not to mistake "kind" with "comfortable." We are sometimes called to share uncomfortable things with others for their own and others' good. For example, we need to point out areas where our subordinates at work need improvement. It would be unkind of us not to do this; who wants to be receiving false and empty praise and affirmation all year, only to be fired for poor performance?

In answering our communal call to holiness, God may also ask us to challenge others at times on their Christian journey. It would be unkind of us to not lovingly confront another if we are aware they have strayed into grievous sin.

We also have to learn how to listen and accept when others point out our own sin in a conflict. God sometimes reveals our logs through others. We need to be able to hear others' observations and concerns about us without resistance and defensiveness. Instead, we can ask ourselves three important questions:

1. What truth might there be in this person's perspective?
2. How can I use this input for my good and the good of others?
3. What is God saying to me in this experience?

Scripture tells us, "...on the day of judgment people will render an account for every careless word they speak" (Mt 12 :36). Take up this particular challenge of The Lesson of the Three Gates for a period of time—perhaps one or two days. See if trying to limit yourself to only true, necessary, and kind communication would bring you any insights. Once you've mastered these three gates, the "extra credit" fourth gate's question is, "Is it uplifting?"

Questions for Reflection & Discussion

1. How do I resist the cultural tendency to blame others and point out their faults during a conflict?

2. Can I think of an example when I consciously relinquished my own will and followed God's will for me in a conflict?

3. When have I successfully confronted another? What specifically helped it to go well? When did I approach another and it did not go well? Why was it unsuccessful?

4. Of the nine strategies to use when confronting others in love, which would I find most difficult to do?

5. Which of these strategies have I used successfully in the past, and how?

6. Which of the three channels of communication do I use most effectively? In which of these channels do I need improvement to make my communication more effective?

Prayer & Reflection

This third step is most difficult;
    it's a tendency I know
To look at other people's sins
    and reach for stones to throw.

I can become so righteous,
    indignant at the sins
Of every person that I see,
    and excuse the sin I'm in!

So help me with compassion, Lord,
    and grow humility in me, too,
So I can look at others,
    and in my heart see only you.

Notes

_____

_____

_____

_____

_____

_____

_____

_____

_____

_____

_____

_____

_____

_____

_____

_____

7

Step Four:
Go and Be Reconciled

Strive for peace with everyone, and for that holiness without which no one will see the Lord. (Heb 12:14)

In our culture, merely achieving a truce or coming to some kind of an agreement reflects an adequate resolution to a conflict. Our faith, however, does not allow us to stop at this. We are expected to seek true healing in the relationship. This usually means seeking forgiveness and being willing to extend it. Scripture tells us,

> As God's chosen ones, holy and beloved, clothe yourselves with compassion, kindness, humility, meekness, and patience. Bear with one another and, if anyone has a complaint against another, forgive each other; just as the Lord has forgiven you, so you also must forgive. (Col 3:12–13)

We are to extend to others the same life-giving forgiveness that Jesus Christ extended to us on the cross. It is only through him that we can reach out to others and achieve deep and lasting reconciliation. We depend on his grace to be able to do what we cannot do ourselves.

An obstacle to achieving true reconciliation is a false idea about what forgiveness is—and what it is not. There are several misconceptions about forgiveness that prevent us from moving forward in healing and restoring relationships broken by conflict (Sande, 206–207). One such misconception is that we need to have feelings of forgiveness before we extend forgiveness to another. If this were true, we might never—or at least not for a very long time—forgive others.

To overcome this misconception, it helps to think of all of the other things we do that we don't necessarily feel like doing. One definition of maturity is acting *in spite* of our feelings rather than *because* of them. It is the same with forgiveness; we are to forgive the other even if we don't feel like it, simply because God has forgiven us first. And as disciples of Jesus we are called to be "ambassadors for Christ" in bringing his reconciliation to the world.

Another misconception is that we don't believe we will ever forget what has happened to us, and so we cannot forgive it. Christians are not expected to forget what has happened to them, but when we extend forgiveness to another, God's grace does begin to affect the degree to which the offense impacts us on a daily basis. It's been said that "Christians forgive to forget" and it is God's grace that moves us toward forgetfulness. In most situations, this grace begins to act as a buffer between our unintentional recollection of the offense and the angry or hurtful feelings we felt when the offense first occurred.

Still another misconception is the notion that forgiving excuses the wrong that was done. Some people think that forgiving is the same as saying, "Don't think anything about it; it was nothing." If it truly were nothing, there would be no need to seek or extend forgiveness. Instead, forgiveness actually acknowledges the wrong that was done. In some cases, restitution may be necessary and there may still be additional consequences to face, even after forgiveness has been granted.

A final misconception of forgiveness is that we think we need to have a guarantee that it's not going to happen again before we forgive. How many of us have ever had to forgive someone for the same offense more than once? More importantly, how many of us have needed forgiveness for the same offense more than once? We are reminded of this in Scripture:

> Then Peter came and said to him, "Lord, if another member of the church sins against me, how often should I forgive? As many as seven times?" Jesus said to him, "Not seven times, but, I tell you, seventy-seven times. (Mt 18:21–22)

In our humanity, it is more common for us to fail in our resolve than to succeed. As St. Paul says, "I do not understand my own actions. For I do not do what I want, but I do the very thing I hate" (Rom 7:15). Yet, like Paul, we find our redemption in Jesus Christ: "Who will rescue me from this body of death? Thanks be to God through Jesus Christ our Lord!" (Rom 7:24–25). As disciples of our redeeming Savior, we are to respond with the same loving generosity and forgiveness towards others that Jesus himself extends to us every day.

Now that we have explored some of the misconceptions about forgiveness, it would be good to look at what forgiveness is. There are many ways to define forgiveness, and we include here examples of what people have shared during our parish mission on Catholic conciliation. One person said that forgiveness is letting go of anger, resentment, and the desire for revenge. Another said that it is letting the other person back into your heart. A third said that it is forever giving up all hope and resentment of ever having a better past. All of these contain essential truths about forgiveness that are important as we seek to heal and restore our relationships.

Still, some people struggle with forgiving others, and nurse grudges long after they can even remember how the conflict originally started. This is not healthy for anyone, spiritually, emotionally, or physically. One last thought, then, on the lack of forgiveness: "Unforgiveness is the poison we drink hoping the other will die."

What would true forgiveness look like? In order for forgiveness to be effective, it would contain four specific elements or promises that we are extending to the person who has offended us. These four promises are:

1. *I will not dwell upon this incident.* Since we cannot control every thought that comes into our head, this refers to entertaining thoughts about the conflict and inflaming all of the emotions we felt when we first experienced the hurt. This is obviously counterproductive if we are trying to forgive and let go of the conflict.

2. *I will not bring up this incident and use it against you.* It has been said that some people get hysterical in conflict while others get historical, dredging up past offenses as ammunition for the current conflict. Committing to this promise means remaining in the present moment and dealing only with the current issues, not reaching into the past to collect arguments against the other.

3. *I will not talk to others about this incident.* Once we have forgiven an offense, we are promising not to disclose the incident to anyone else. There is sometimes a great temptation to commiserate with someone who has suffered a similar offense at the hands of the same person who had hurt us. But when we forgive, we are vowing not to give in to that temptation. Note, too, that choosing not to spread the incident to others after we have extended forgiveness to the person is not the same as seeking another's wisdom in the midst of a conflict to learn better how to handle it. We frequently do need to seek advice or counsel from people just to learn how to navigate successfully through turbulent times. The key differences are in the motivation and intent of our sharing.

4. *I will not allow this incident to stand between us or hinder our personal relationship.* As we move into the future with the person we have forgiven, and as difficult as it may be, we are promising to allow trust to develop again between us. We will decide not to avoid situations that place us in the posi-

tion of possibly being hurt again, as long as these are not physically or emotionally abusive situations. Instead, we will trust God to bring about the healing in the relationship that will result in true reconciliation.

It is worth noting here that these four promises apply to ourselves as well as to others. We are often our own worst enemies, continually recalling our own shortcomings and condemning ourselves for the mistakes we've made. How wonderful to promise ourselves that the past will be accepted for what it was, and that today is a new day, full of promise, opportunity, and especially, God's grace.

It is also good to note that if we are serious about the promises of forgiveness, we should not forgive prematurely. That is, we need to be sure that we are willing to follow through on these promises and not just relegate forgiveness to lip service. Rather than forgiving someone before we are able to commit to these promises, it would be better to explain just what forgiveness means to us and that we are working toward that goal.

Being willing to follow through with the difficult work of forgiveness requires much prayer, and trust in God's grace. In a conflict, it often takes us a long time to calm down, recognize our contribution to a dispute, and become willing to acknowledge our fault to the other person. But we know that using the four-step process of Catholic conciliation—a profoundly simple though challenging process—significantly increases the chances of reaching true and lasting reconciliation.

We have witnessed dramatic conversions of heart as the Holy Spirit has led people to reach out to others with whom they have been embroiled in bitter and protracted disputes. We know that we do not do this on our own power; as Catholics we are called to depend on God's strength. It is in Jesus Christ that we can grant others forgiveness and desire true reconciliation. And it is only in him that this is possible.

"The struggle for mercy goes on unceasingly in our hearts," says Fr. Servais Pindaers, OP, professor of moral theology at the University of Fribourg, Switzerland. What a beautiful struggle to continually offer up to our God, in whose heart there is no struggle for the mercy he continues to shower upon us in every moment of our lives. When we face God in our own moment of judgment, we would we rather hear him say, "You forgave too much" rather than, "You judged too much."

We are called to be witnesses of Christ's love and to be his apostles of reconciliation in the world. Let us remember our individual call to holiness and live it out in every circumstance of life, especially when we find ourselves in interpersonal conflict. Availing ourselves of frequent reception of the sacrament of reconciliation will give us the necessary grace to remain in a disposition of conciliation.

May the words of St. Francis of Assisi be an inspiration and help to us:

Lord, make me an instrument of your peace.
Where there is hatred, let me sow love;
   where there is injury, pardon;
   where there is doubt, faith;
   where there is despair, hope;

If we take a careful look at the movements of our heart we will quickly perceive that every day brings countless occasions for practicing mercy and forgiveness, not so much because of injustices done to us as because of our own propensity for judging the conduct of others according to our impressions. The slightest dis-agreement, word, tone of voice, or gesture, is enough to start a series of judgments and to confront us with the question of justice and mercy. The beatitude of the merciful is offered to us daily as we choose between a justice that suits our impressionable and often preemptory taste, and a generous, kind, and understanding justice. The struggle for mercy goes on unceasingly in our hearts.

—Fr. Servais Pindaers, OP

where there is darkness, light;
where there is sadness, joy.

O, Divine Master, grant that I may not
    so much seek to be consoled as to console;
    to be understood as to understand;
    to be loved as to love;
For it is in giving that we receive;
    it is in pardoning that we are pardoned;
    it is in dying that we are born again
     to eternal life.

Questions for Reflection & Discussion

1. What prevents me from forgiving others when they wrong me or those I love?

2. Which of the misconceptions about forgiveness have I believed?

3. Which of the four promises of forgiveness will I find most difficult to make?

4. Can I think of any examples where the "struggle for mercy" was present in my heart?

Prayer & Reflection

Whenever conflict rages,
    we seek to justify our thoughts;
We say we'll carry to the grave
    the things for which we've fought.

And God has no dispute with this;
    it is our death that he would like:
We need to put to death our will
    and the reasons that we fight!

We're truly called to leave behind
    all that we want for self,
Seeking the good of others,
    and putting our wills upon the shelf.

True healing is God's wisdom
    for every fight we're in,
Relying on his grace and love
    to overcome our sin.

So cast down all self interest
    and put aside your rights for him
And he will bring true healing
    to every conflict you are in.

Notes

8

Making Peace

The feud had been going on for years. Jack couldn't remember when it had started exactly or why. Oh, it was probably like a lot of fights: misunderstandings turning into angry words, hurt feelings, the heat of the moment changed into an icy standoff with neither one willing to make the first move to reconcile. Both parties feeling justified in their pain, both too proud to seek the other out. It was probably like a lot of families who had emotional arguments turn into long-term feuds. "From the heat of the battle to our own cold war," Jack mused.

His estrangement from Peggy, his older sister by three years, had been more and more on his mind lately, and he wasn't sure why. Maybe it was because of the pictures. A few weeks ago, one of his grandchildren needed some photographs of the family for a school project, something about making a family tree. Jack had hauled some boxes out of the attic and had been going through them trying to find some that they could part with—because you were never sure whether you'd ever see them again once they were put on poster board and taken to school!

Maybe it was because another birthday had passed, usually times of great family fun, and he hadn't heard a word from Peggy. Not that he'd expected to. He didn't acknowledge her birthdays, either. They hadn't spoken at all now for twelve years.

Jack guessed that if he thought hard enough about it, he could replay the original argument, but he didn't have the interest anymore. Whenever he thought about it, he felt petty, small, and ashamed. It sure wasn't something that deserved twelve years of hurt and anger; he knew that.

What he didn't know was how to end it. His wife, Mary, had urged him to call Peggy a few days after the argument, but he was still angry, still thinking that she had hurt him and she should be the one to call. She never did, and then it was too awkward for him—and they froze in their feelings and their positions—for the next twelve years.

The family get-togethers had been strained at first with a lot of tension and everyone conscious of when he and Peggy were in the same room. But after awhile, the family kind of grew around the fight, like the body making an adjustment to a wound. It was there—a place of injury and pain—but everyone and everything went on despite it, adjusting to it, allowing for it, and finally accepting and ignoring it.

Lent had been particularly difficult for Jack since the argument. All of the readings every year spoke of repentance for sin, of examining your conscience and rooting out everything that separates you from God and one another. The very first thing that always popped into Jack's mind each time the priest spoke about sin was his fight with Peggy. Up to now he'd been able to rationalize and defend his position, but he just didn't have the energy for it anymore—and he'd stopped believing his reasoning anyway.

This was the first time, though, that he finally had a sense that he knew how to end it.

"Before it's too late," Jack thought, echoing the words of the priest in his homily during the Ash Wednesday Mass. The priest spoke about a seminar he had attended on peacemaking. He shared the four steps in the process, and he shared a very personal story of how he had reconciled with his brother after seventeen years of not speaking to him. Jack was moved by the old priest's story, and by his willingness to tell his people about it.

The priest had begun with the words, "I'm not who you think I am." He spoke of the lack of forgiveness in his heart, of his pride and self-righteousness, and of his stubbornness. He spoke of the pain of the argument with his brother, and the greater pain of feeling like a hypocrite as he preached one thing to his people and lived another in his life.

Jack was sure that many people felt the same way he did as the priest talked; they were just like him. They, too, could see gaps in their own lives between their "talk" and their "walk." The priest said to them, "I realized that if my Christianity didn't work at home, I shouldn't export it. I realized that our God is a God of unity; right before his passion, Jesus prayed, 'that they may all be one. As you, Father, are in me and I am in you, may they also be in us...'" (Jn 17:21).

The priest then spoke of how he had applied the four steps of the peacemaking process to the situation with his brother. It wasn't easy, but it began the healing of their relationship, and their family was reunited again. The story left Jack choked up because whenever the priest spoke of his brother, of their happy past together, of their painful estrangement, and now their joyful reconciliation, Jack thought of Peggy.

The old priest wiped his eyes as he encouraged his people to search their hearts and ask God to unite what they have allowed Satan to divide. "Before it's too late," he had said, "before death intervenes and regret rules your life."

Jack sat holding his favorite picture of his childhood. It was a candid shot that his mother had taken when he was about eleven. He was sitting at the dining room table with schoolbooks scattered around him and a look of utter bewilderment on his face; learning never came easy for him. Peggy—at that awkward age between childhood and adolescence—was next to him, pointing at something in a book, encouraging him, teaching him, supporting him, as she had always done all through his growing up.

Jack got out of his chair and picked up the phone. He had been thinking enough about the past; he decided to do something about the future.

Questions for Reflection & Discussion

1. Write a letter to someone with whom you have an unresolved conflict, applying the principles of Catholic peacemaking. This letter is not to be mailed, but would provide an opportunity to use the principles in a real-life situation. (This exercise may also lay the foundation for a future reconciliation.)

2. Select a favorite saint or biblical character who, in your opinion, exhibited many of these peacemaking principles in their life. Why did you select this person, and how can their example be relevant to your own life?

3. Frequently, as we become familiar with the concepts of Catholic peacemaking, the Holy Spirit brings to mind someone with whom we are in conflict. If this has been your experience, commit to praying daily for this person for at least one week. "Bless those who persecute you; bless and do not curse them" (Rom 12:14).

4. Share what you have learned about Catholic peacemaking with three other people during the next week. Be prepared to discuss the personal impact this knowledge has had in your life.

Prayer & Reflection

If then there is any encouragement in Christ, any consolation from love, any sharing in the Spirit, any compassion and sympathy, make my joy complete: be of the same mind, having the same love, being in full accord and of one mind. Do nothing from selfish ambition or conceit, but in humility regard others as better than yourselves. Let each of you look not to your own interests, but to the interests of others. Let the same mind be in you that was in Christ Jesus, who, though he was in the form of God, did not regard equality with God as something to be exploited, but emptied himself, taking the form of a slave, being born in human likeness. And being found in human form, he humbled himself and became obedient to the point of death—even death on a cross (Phil 2:1–8).

Notes

_____

_____

_____

_____

_____

_____

_____

Bibliography

Baltimore Catechism. 1891 and 1921. New York, NY: Benziger Brothers. HTML translation, 1995. Catholic Information Center on Internet, Inc.

Broderick, Robert C., ed. *The Catholic Encyclopedia.* Nashville, TN: Thomas Nelson, Inc., 1987.

Catechism of the Catholic Church (CCC). Liguori, MO; Liguori Publications, 1994.

Code of Canon Law. Washington, DC, Canon Law Society of America, 1984.

Flannery, Austin, OP. *Vatican Council II: The Conciliar and Post Conciliar Documents.* New York, NY: Costello Publishing Company, Inc., 1975.

Sande, Ken. *The Peacemaker.* Grand Rapids, MI: Baker Books, 1997.

Saint Joseph Daily Missal. New York, NY: Catholic Book Publishing Company, 1959.

Senge, Peter M., et al. *The Fifth Discipline Fieldbook.* New York, NY: Doubleday, 1994.

United States Conference of Catholic Bishops. *Procedures for Resolving Conflict.* Washington, DC: United States Conference of Catholic Bishops, 2002.